SOMETHING SPECIAL WITHIN

DeVorss & Company, Publishers

Fifth Printing, 1990

ISBN: 0-87516-488-9
Library of Congress Card Catalog No.: 78-69983

DeVorss & Company, Publisher
P.O. Box 550
Marina del Rey, CA 90294

Printed in The United States of America

SOMETHING SPECIAL WITHIN

Story . . . . Betts Richter
Illustration and Design . . . . Alice Jacobsen
Graphics Consulting . . . . Jack Tipple

Many thanks to those who so graciously gave assistance and direction in putting together this book, our first effort. We can never fully give credit to everyone. The following are but a few of the gracious, loving persons who have given of their time, talents and wise counsel.

Thank you to:
Walt Rugani, Angela Japor, Richard Lang, Rev. Barbara Thomas, Rev. Carol Ruth Knox, Debbie Rozman, Christopher Hills, Swami Kriyananda, Carole Swain, Dr. Lornie Grinton and the creative source within each of us.

Dedicated gratefully
to all our teachers
each day of our lives

and

to Marlo and Angele

There is something
very special
within you

waiting for your joy
of **discovery**.

It is the place within you
where love lives.

3

You know it's there when you hold
a soft cuddly kitten or puppy,
or someone you love;

and you feel a warm,
velvety feeling inside
that we call love.

It warms you through and through
much like the sun does.

When you close your eyes
and think of the sun
you can imagine a light.
We call that your love-light.

Whenever you like or love yourself,
  or someone,
  or a pet,
  or even a tiny flower or rock,

You feel that love-light
  inside you.

And you feel
warm, happy and joyful.

The more you practice loving,
the more love-light you feel,
and the more it grows.

Then people around you feel good, too,
    and they respond to you
    in a warm, loving way.

Sometimes others are unkind
and then you feel hurt, angry,
or mixed up.

They act that way because
    their love-light is weak,
And they don't like themselves
    very much.

Sometimes your love-light gets dim
because of sad things
that happen in your life.
Then it's hard to remember
the special person you are.

When you are sad, lonely,
    afraid, or angry,
there are ways to
    keep your love-light shining
    and help it grow stronger,
    more sure and more beautiful.

How?
It really isn't hard at all.
Here are some easy things to do
    to help your love-light grow.

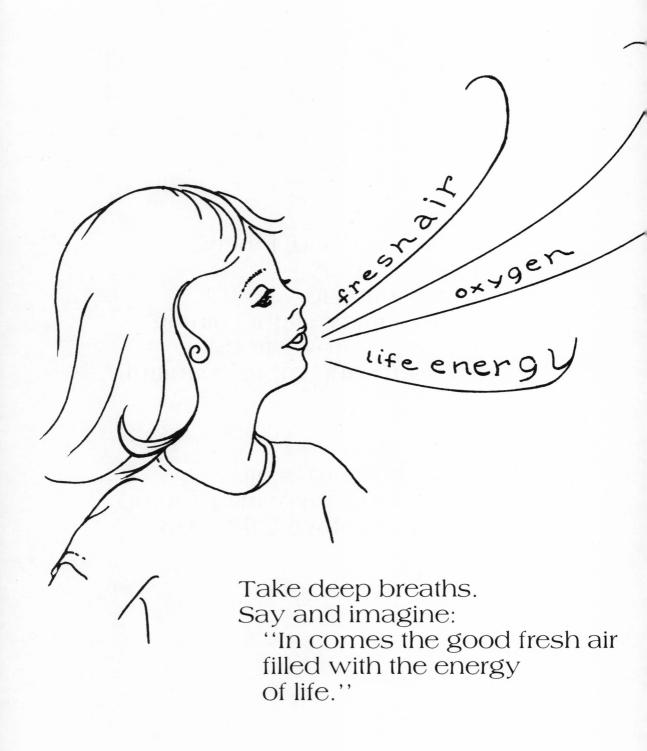

Take deep breaths.
Say and imagine:
    "In comes the good fresh air
    filled with the energy
    of life."

"Out goes all the sadness,
loneliness, fear, and anger."

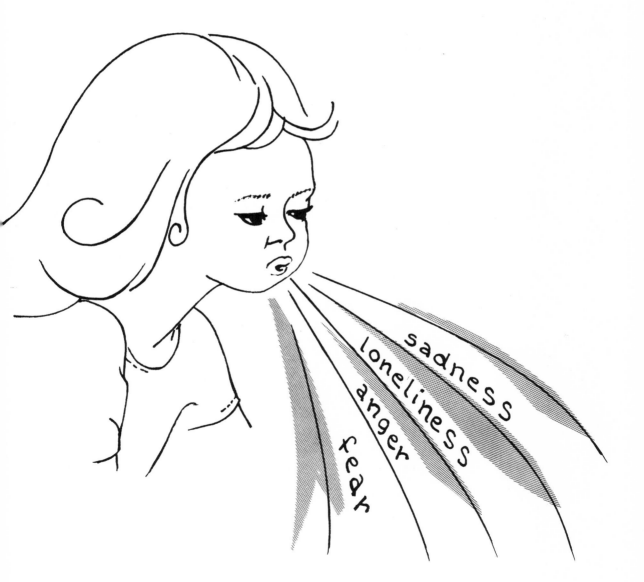

When it's awfully hard
   to think of your own love-light,
   it might help if you —

Imagine that you have an angel
   enfolding you
   with its golden-white light
   and holding you
   until you feel strong again.

21

Think of your love-light often.
Be aware of the
   warm glow
   inside you.

Say and imagine:
   "My love-light shines inside me.
   I feel warm and happy."

Know that you are a **very special person.**
You are **unique!** (You are one of a kind.)

No one is exactly like you.

Enjoy the many ways you are different.

Know that you are a miracle.

Everything about you is perfect,
   and works together for you
   without you thinking about it at all.

You see the beauties of nature,
You hear the sounds
 of the birds and the wind,
 your family and friends.

You smell the delicious odors
of Mom's good cooking,

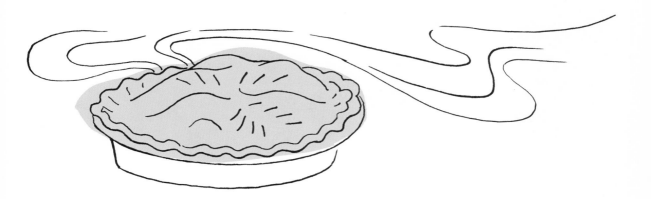

and you feel the tender touch of love.

You don't have to think about it.
Your body just does it.

You run in the sunshine
breathing the fresh clean air
without telling your body how.

Your body uses the nourishing food you eat to build strong bones and muscles without saying anything to it.

And so much more!

Say:

"I am a miracle."

"I am truly special."

Everyone is a miracle of life
and unique.

And the more you know about others,

the more you see of yourself

in each one of them.

And the more you look,
    the more you will see
    the love-light in each person.

As you become aware of the love-light
    in others,
    your happiness grows.

Share hugs with people
    you love.

Love is something
    that grows within you
    as you give it away.

It's strange but true:
    the more love you give,
    the more love you have.

Practice feeling joyful.

Spend as much time
    as you can
    with happy, loving people.

Sing happy songs.
Sing from your heart.
Listen to happy music.
    Move to it.

Dance in any way
that feels good to you.

In the morning
    think of the happy things
    you want to happen.
Imagine them happening for you
    and notice how it feels.

This will help them happen.

At the end of the day
    think of all the happy things
    that did happen.

Write them in a special book.

HAPPY THINGS Book

The sun shined today.

I saw a funny bug today.

I did my work quickly and well.

Someone smiled back at me.

I smelled a beautiful flower today. I got all the way across the bars today.

Now you know some easy ways
to help your love-light grow.

1. Take deep breaths.
2. Think of your love-light.
   3. Know the special person you are.
   4. Share hugs with those you love.
   5. Be with happy, loving people.
   6. Enjoy happy music.
7. Imagine good things happening.
8. Write happy things that did happen.

Do these things often and your love-light
will grow, and grow and grow.